NEW VANGUARD 219

RIOT CONTROL VEHICLES

1945–Present

CHRIS McNAB   ILLUSTRATED BY IAN PALMER

First published in Great Britain in 2015 by Osprey Publishing,
PO Box 883, Oxford, OX1 9PL, UK
PO Box 3985, New York, NY 10185-3985, USA
E-mail: info@ospreypublishing.com

Osprey Publishing is part of the Osprey Group

A CIP catalogue record for this book is available from the British Library

Print ISBN: 978 1 4728 0515 7
PDF ebook ISBN: 978 1 4728 0516 4
ePub ebook ISBN: 978 1 4728 0517 1

Index by Zoe Ross
Typeset in Sabon and Myriad Pro
Originated by PDQ Media, Bungay, UK
Printed in China through World Print Ltd.

15 16 17 18 19   10 9 8 7 6 5 4 3 2 1

Osprey Publishing is supporting the Woodland Trust, the UK's leading
woodland conservation charity, by funding the dedication of trees.

www.ospreypublishing.com

ACKNOWLEDGEMENTS

The author would like to thank all those at the Paramount Group who
helped with the research and photographs of this book, especially Nico
de Clerk, Jason Bronkurst and Len Mellett, Head of Innovation, for his
fascinating interview. I would also like to thank Maria Tkacheva of INKAS
for providing me with additional photos. Final thanks go to Tom Milner at
Osprey for his help in steering this book through to print.

CONTENTS

INTRODUCTION   **4**

DESIGN AND DEVELOPMENT   **6**
- Armoured Cars and Specialist Police Vehicles 1890–1945
- Offensive Weapons
- Cold-War Era RCVs
- Military Armoured Vehicles as RCVs

**EXPLORING VARIANTS – BRITISH RCVS IN
NORTHERN IRELAND**   **15**
- International Developments

MODERN VARIANTS – STATE OF THE ART   **26**

OPERATIONAL HISTORY   **34**

CONCLUSION   **46**

FURTHER READING   **47**

INDEX   **48**

RIOT CONTROL VEHICLES
1945–PRESENT

INTRODUCTION

The story of riot-control vehicles (RCVs) is not the simple evolution of a single type. The narrative is complicated by the fact that the definition of 'riot-control vehicle' can depend as much on context as on the nature of the vehicle itself. For example, during the explosive riots in the 1960s in the United States, National Guard M113 armoured personnel carriers (APCs) were deployed to patrol the streets, demolish barricades and provide some measure of crowd control. In these circumstances, the M113s were de facto RCVs, despite the fact that they were not designed for this specific purpose. Indeed, throughout the history of RCVs, we find that the lines between APC, armoured car, infantry fighting vehicle (IFV) and even main battle tank can blur with the category of RCV, depending on the purpose to which the vehicle is put.

On this basis, almost every military vehicle can be classed as an RCV, if it is used specifically for crowd control. Such a position in this book would lead

Fire remains one of the most dangerous weapons deployed by rioters. Here a Bahraini armoured police vehicle burns in Jidhafs, Bahrain, on the outskirts of the capital of Manama, following violent clashes in 2012.
(Press Association)

to an unmanageably expansive account. For this reason, the focus here is primarily on those vehicles that have been designed from the outset as RCVs, or which have been given a specific set of modifications to fulfil the RCV role. Still, the variety of vehicles is huge. They range from armoured cars crudely fitted with bull bars and tear-gas dispensers, through to futuristic riot trucks fitted with fully computerized anti-riot and surveillance systems. Some are little more than civilian vehicles with basic protection, whereas others wouldn't look out of place on a battlefield. Furthermore, RCVs can belong in either the military or the law-enforcement domains (although more typically the latter), and as such their design and capabilities reflect the priorities of those different communities.

So what are the common characteristics of an RCV? In essence, an RCV is a vehicle capable of both controlling and simultaneously surviving aggressive crowds. The offensive technologies it deploys as part of the vehicle are principally (but not always) non-lethal in type – water cannon and tear gas are the traditional favourites, but more futuristic options include sonic blasts and microwave beams. The survivability aspect of an RCV is critical. Riotous crowds may appear chaotic, but they also have a formidable group intelligence, and will use every resource at their disposal to destroy a vehicular threat. These resources include thrown rocks, crowbars and other impact tools, fireworks, petrol bombs, explosives and firearms. Thus every aspect of the RCV must be designed to survive the creative destruction of a large crowd. Windows must be hardened against fracture; bodywork should shrug off missiles; tyres should be resistant to puncturing and fire; fire prevention needs to be inbuilt; occupants need to make their entrance and exit quickly and safely, and they require all-round surveillance to spot emerging threats; the cabin areas should be climate controlled and resistant to gas and smoke. Any vehicle that does not have a stable wheelbase is likely to be rocked over onto its back. A single chink in the vehicle's protection will be ruthlessly exposed in the mêlée of a riot.

RCVs have had far less coverage in books and magazines than military armoured vehicles, and yet RCVs are, in a sense, the most combat-tested of vehicles. Almost every nation in the world has experienced civil disturbances,

A protestor in Valparaiso, Chile, hurls a rock at a police armoured car. The vehicle is actually the Mahindra Marksman, an Indian-produced vehicle with armour capable of handling small-arms fire and even grenade attacks. (Press Association)

some bordering on outright conflict, and RCVs plunge into these on virtually a weekly basis around the world. The occupants of these vehicles depend upon the RCV for their very survival, and this alone makes them a worthy subject of study.

DESIGN AND DEVELOPMENT

An early object lesson in the vulnerability of unprotected police vehicles to rioters. An Egyptian police car burns after being overturned and set on fire by rioters in the Square of Mehemet Ali, July 1930. (Press Association)

The history of the design and development of RCVs is neither a linear nor even a particularly logical affair, as variations in approaches to RCV design vary considerably from country to country. If we were to identify two key trends, however, they would be these: 1) RCVs created simply by modifying existing civilian, police or military vehicles; and 2) purpose-designed RCVs, created specifically for the job in hand.

With these two contexts in mind, this history focuses mainly on the period from the end of World War II until the present day. It was in the aftermath of the war and during the social and political turbulence of the 1950s–80s that RCVs emerged in earnest, as police and military forces attempted to develop more technologically authoritative responses to civic strife. There are, however, some pre-1945 precedents worth consideration.

Armoured Cars and Specialist Police Vehicles 1890–1945

In many ways the RCV is the intersection between the armoured car and the police vehicle. The first armoured cars – disregarding some of the mechanical improbabilities of the 18th and much of the 19th centuries – emerged in the late 1890s, but it was World War I that galvanized their development and production, not only for combat, but also for colonial policing duties. Rolls-Royce, for example, took the chassis of the classic Silver Ghost and utilized it to form a robust-looking armoured car, protected by up to 12mm of armour plate and armed with a .303in Vickers machine gun in a turret. The 7,428cc straight-six engine delivered a top speed of up to 72km/h. The Mk 1 armoured car emerged in December 1914, and variants of the vehicle were in service until 1944. The Rolls-Royce was by no means a dedicated riot-control vehicle, but it found utility in policing the volatile streets of Egypt and Palestine, and Northern Ireland during the Irish Civil War (1922–23) in the hands of the Irish Free State.

Even as armoured cars evolved, another development was beginning in the world of law enforcement. As with armoured vehicles, police vehicles began to emerge in the late 19th century, but did not really reach a satisfying degree of sophistication until the 1920s. The internal-combustion engine revolution offered police forces around the world, but especially in the United States, the means to respond more rapidly to emergency events. The Prohibition era (1920–23) and its associated gangsterism provided a ready incentive for the motorization of police units. When equipped with a radio, the cars enabled police departments to cover larger areas of ground using fewer manpower commitments. The international leader in this regard was the New York City Police Department, which adopted an entire fleet of radio-equipped cars in 1920. Yet the 1920s and 1930s were also a time of civil disturbances sweeping the United States, hence we also witness the emergence of what we would classify as purpose-specific riot-control vehicles.

A particularly enlightening article in this regard is found in the May 1938 edition of *Mechanics and Handicraft*. The cover of the magazine displays a rather sci-fi-looking illustration of a 'riot truck', operated by ominous gas-mask-wearing personnel. The vehicle – designed and patented by Brooklyn citizen Victorino L. Tunaya – is painted in the most lurid of reds, and looks somewhat akin to an express train fitted with gas, water and machine-gun turrets. While the layout of the vehicle is somewhat outlandish, the core principles of the RCV are all there. The text that accompanies the artwork inside the magazine explains the vehicle's properties:

> This vehicle is provided with a number of discharge nozzles through which powerful streams of water or liquid gas can be projected on rioting groups of persons. In event of very serious trouble, machine guns may be mounted in the turrets instead of hose nozzles to deal with rioters with greater finality. Two huge tanks contain the liquid, which is driven through nozzles by a pump.
> *Mechanics and Handicraft*, May 1938

What the article describes is essentially an armoured RCV with multiple lethal and non-lethal threat responses. The personnel manning the vehicle are shown protected behind the armoured bodywork and their turrets. Although the vehicle is essentially impractical (its long six-wheel design would deliver poor manoeuvrability in city streets, for example), the patented design shows that the RCV was a defined concept just prior to World War II. Furthermore, while the 'Riot Truck' remained on paper, around the world actual examples of operational vehicles were emerging.

A re-enactment group conduct a patrol in a vintage Rolls-Royce Armoured Car. The Rolls-Royce was used for various colonial policing duties, and it had a potent force option in the form of a turret-mounted Vickers .303 machine gun. (Simon Q)

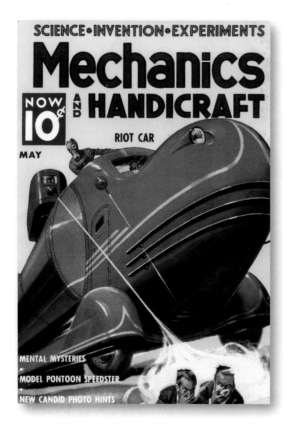

The cover of *Mechanics and Handicraft* in May 1938 showed a new vision – the riot car. Although to modern eyes it has a rather 'Buck Rogers' appearance, it embodies the key considerations of an RCV – a protected body, good observation and a range of defensive options.

In 1930, New York City created its Emergency Service Division (ESU), dedicated to handling all manner of civic crises, including riots. To facilitate this role, the ESU was equipped with emergency trucks. To modern eyes, they look largely like fire trucks – principally open-top four-wheel Mack trucks, with rescue ladders mounted on each side of the body. Photographs show an open cab for the driver and co-driver protected behind a simple one-piece rectangular windscreen. (An angled visor running along the top edge of the windscreen offers some protection from hand-thrown missiles.) Behind them the truck body features bench seating for around ten occupants, with an emergency bell and searchlight set at the front of the truck, plus a mounting for a Thompson .45-cal sub-machine gun just behind the cab. Further photos show multiple officers presenting their weapons over the sides of the truck, using the side ladders like a parapet to steady the mix of sub-machine guns and pump-action shotguns.

During the 1930s and 40s the NYPD realized – doubtless from hard experience – that well-armed occupants were no substitute for a well-protected cab. The ESU consequently upgraded their trucks to receive protective bodies. A 1945 issue of *Public Safety* features an article on the latest varieties of 'Bus-Type Emergency Truck'. The article explains that

The typical modern emergency vehicle of the New York Police Department is a streamlined 15-ton, Model WA-122 White super power truck with cab-over engine design, geared to travel up to seventy miles an hour. This is an all-enclosed job, painted in the police colours of green and white, and equipped with automatic warning signals... The various items of equipment are neatly stowed away in protective compartments where they can be reached easily. Included aboard are squad accommodations, four floodlights of 1,000 candle power, portable telephone and 1,000 feet of wire which can be strung at the scene of a disaster, two-way radio, 100-volt generator to power the lights and other electrical equipment, inhalators, rifles, fire axes, jacks, nets, poles, ladders, and other tools.

Public Safety, October 1945

In many ways, the ESU vehicle resembles a camper van in layout, albeit with more protection and specialist equipment inside. Although it was purposed for many civic emergencies, not just riots, its contents illustrate how an effective RCV must be more than just armour and non-lethal weaponry.

The British were also finding that truck conversions were an ideal route to relatively cheap RCVs. Some good examples of early British RCVs can be found in post-war colonial outposts. In Hong Kong, for example, the authorities deployed Commer trucks heavily converted to the RCV role. Commer had manufactured a range of civilian and military trucks, and the Hong Kong Police took a Q4 cab-behind-engine truck and wrapped it in a metal shell, with an observation/fire turret positioned on the top. Although the vehicle was a conversion, rather than a new design, it incorporated some modern features. The bodywork had very smooth angles at the transitions between panels, which would help the vehicle survive missile impacts and better cope with flammable fluid attacks. The vision slots set into this body – two in each side and one next to the driver and co-driver – were extremely small in order to keep the vehicle's vulnerabilities to a minimum. The engine was heavily covered with an armoured hood, protecting the vehicle's powerplant from any immobilizing attacks. The hood was heavily ventilated with slots on all sides, ensuring that the engine got plenty of cooling air in order to avoid overheating. Capacious metal wheel arches provided a boxed-over protection down to half the tyre depth, and the windows had folding shutters hinged to the top frame, these being closed up once the missiles started flying.

Many of the early RCVs did not feature integral non-lethal weaponry, a key difference from those that exist today. However, over time the non-lethal options would increase, emphasizing dispersal and control rather than delivering potentially mortal wounds.

Offensive Weapons

Understanding the development of RCVs post-1945 requires a brief overview of the core range of options for on-board weaponry. RCVs are principally tasked with the job of crowd dispersal and control, and if the crowd actively resists that aim, then the vehicle must compel them through force.

Traditionally there have been three principal types of weapon fitted on RCVs – water, gas and pyrotechnic devices. (Rubber bullets are also used, but they tend to be fired more from hand-held weapons, not vehicular mounts.) Note that all of these are weapons of the non-lethal variety; a true RCV is generally not in the business of killing people, although many states have

Istanbul, 2014. A Turkish Police RCV opens fire with its water cannon; the vehicle is an RCV adaptation of the Cadillac Gage V-100 Commando, a US armoured fighting vehicle. Note the extendible shield at the front of the hull. (Press Association)

deployed military armoured cars and APCs against their people to do just that. The primary intention behind the deployment of the weapon is instead, according to the US Army's *Civil Disturbances* field manual, to 'distract, deter, or disable disorderly people' with weapon effects that are 'temporary and disappear within minutes of exposure'.

The archetypal riot-control weapon is the water cannon. Water cannon have several levels of effect on a crowd. First, the simple act of soaking alone can dampen a riot. People are often less ardent in their passions when their clothing is sodden, particularly in cooler climates where they might experience significant and rapid heat loss. Then there is the impact of the jet itself. Water cannon can hit like a fist, the high-velocity jet literally knocking people off their feet or causing bruising and low-level impact injuries. (In some instances, the water jet can even strip off clothing.) Such a jet can carve through a concentrated crowd like a knife, making the rioters more open to dispersal by riot-control troops or RCV movement.

Since the 1950s, riot-control agents (RCAs) have also been a popular crowd-control tool. Under the RCA banner come a variety of chemical agents, including CS gas and CR spray, and together they deliver a host of unpleasant symptoms such as eye irritation, temporary blindness, respiratory distress, skin irritation and vomiting. During riots, gas is frequently deployed by ground troops or dismounted police officers firing gas canisters from hand-held launchers. Yet RCVs are also an ideal platform for dispensing gas grenades from dedicated multiple-launch units typically mounted on the front and sides of the vehicle. RCVs (particularly modern varieties) have the advantage that the occupants of the vehicle are partially or fully protected from the gas they deploy, unlike foot soldiers, who can find themselves choking on the gas if the wind happens to be blowing in the wrong direction. RCVs can also have dedicated turrets for dispensing irritant sprays.

Note that although CS gas is by far the most common gas munition launched from the grenade dispensers of RCVs, it is not the only option. Many launchers can be pre-loaded with a selection of munition types, including stun grenades (ground burst or air burst) and anti-riot fragmentation grenades, which dispense non-lethal rubber pellets instead of lethal metallic fragments.

Armoured cars provided the first crude options for riot control. Here we see a German armoured car policing the streets of Kiev, Ukraine, following the departure of Russia from World War I in 1917. (Press Association)

Beyond water, gas, sprays and grenades, we are today moving into new territories for vehicle-mounted riot-control weapons. The force options now include directed-energy devices such as the US Active Denial System (ADS), which via an energy beam imparts a severe sensation of burning and an uncontrollable desire to flee. There are also various sonic and ultrasound weapons (SUWs) in development, which can induce nausea, visual distortion or even a loss of bowel control in the unfortunate troublemakers. Such devices are explored in more detail below, but they illustrate the fact that non-lethal options are ever-broadening.

One final point to remember is that RCVs can also deploy a range of psychological tools, aside from the natural visual intimidation of the vehicle itself. Powerful searchlights can unnerve all those who are caught in their steady beam – as can video surveillance devices on modern vehicles – while loudspeakers deliver a steady stream of pre-recorded or live broadcasts to dissuade the crowd from their course of action.

Cold-War Era RCVs Water Cannon

In many ways, water-cannon vehicles are the true progenitors of the modern RCV, as they combine crew protection with non-lethal offensive capability in a single unit. The earliest example of a water-cannon vehicle, and probably of an RCV in general, was seen on the riotous streets of Berlin in 1931. The sophistication of this early vehicle is impressive. It is built around a Mercedes truck chassis and cab, the flatbed replaced by an enclosed cabin containing the water tank plus a rotating turret on the top holding the water-jet nozzle. Power for the water pump came directly from the engine. As water-cannon technology progressed during the inter-war period, the water pumps of these vehicles would increasingly be independent of the engine, allowing them to deliver water without the weapon depriving the engine of force.

Water cannon emerged more prolifically in the post-1945 period, especially in Eastern Europe and the Soviet Union, with all their associated post-war security issues. At first the Soviets adopted the riot-control solution favoured by many nations – in the absence of specialist vehicles, they simply wheeled out fire-service vehicles and turned the hoses on the protesters. Yet for reasons explained in more detail below, such vehicles were far from ideal for riot conditions, and so the Soviet and Eastern European authorities turned to producing more specialized vehicles.

In post-war East Berlin, for example, there emerged the 'Socialist Water Jet'. This was an RCV based on the IFA G5 truck. The G5 was a three-axle vehicle produced in East Germany between 1952 and 1964 and put to various purposes including as a military supply truck, a fire engine and, in its SK-2 variation, as a water cannon. The base vehicle had a six-cylinder 120hp diesel engine with a five-speed gearbox and a maximum road speed of 80km/h; the driver could switch between six-wheel and four-wheel drive as required. To convert the truck into the SK-2, the cab and engine received an armoured cover, the windows were given protective shutters, a water tank was fitted to the rear and a top-mounted revolving turret held the water-jet nozzle. Usefully, the vehicle also had a central tyre-pressure adjustment system, allowing the driver to alter the pressure according to the terrain or the obstacles he had to negotiate.

The SK-2 was an early vehicle amongst an increasingly advanced fleet of water-cannon vehicles produced within the Soviet Bloc. Throughout the

1960s, 1970s and 1980s, RCVs upped their sophistication and levels of crowd influence. Within Russia, the Soviet authorities made a range of water cannon on military MAZ chassis, while in the 1970s Poland created the first in the series of excellent Hydromil vehicles. In the Hydromil II format, which entered production in 1983, the vehicle features a fully grill-enclosed cabin and rear crew compartment and has two top-mounted water-jet nozzles, each individually directable. The chassis is produced by Jelcz and the power is supplied by a 413hp engine driving all four wheels. The vehicles of the Hydromil stable have been in frequent use since the 1960s, and they also achieved export success throughout the Soviet Bloc.

Shown in communist-era livery for show purposes, a Polish Police Jelcz Hydromil II rolls along a Polish avenue in 2006. The Hydromil II was produced from 1983, and had an 8,000-litre water tank. (Now)

The Paramount Group Maverick is a cutting-edge security vehicle. Windows and bodywork are protected to cope with 7.62x54mm rounds and under-belly grenade attacks, and a turreted observation block on the roof provides excellent all-round surveillance. (Paramount Group)

The West was somewhat slower than the East in developing its fleet of water-cannon RCVs. In Europe, the police and military tended to go down the route of fire engine or truck conversions. In West Germany in the 1950s, for example, the police took the Magirus Mercur fire engine, with its 600-gallon-per-minute water pump, and added protective features to make it suitable for use as an RCV. In the late 1960s the British purchased a new generation of water cannon from the German manufacturer Mayer, based in Hagen, Westphalia. It was reported that the jet from these vehicles was sufficient to knock a man off his feet at a range of nearly 30m, and have a bludgeoning effect out to 40m. The chassis on which other vehicles were constructed were diverse – Mercedes, Magirus, MAN, Ford, Bussing – but common features took hold. These included a fully protected cab and crew compartment, multiple directable water jets, variable water-pressure systems and also the ability to introduce irritants or dyes into the water flow, to increase the crowd-dispersal effect.

Looking across the Atlantic to the United States, readily available water cannon for most US states have traditionally been simple water hoses, rigged up to a hydrant or operated from the back of a truck. Such a crowd-dispersal instrument was especially popular during the 1950s and 1960s in the United States, against striking workers or civil-rights protesters. Yet the application of fire-service equipment to civic disorders is rarely recommended. Fire trucks themselves have little in the way of protective features for riot conditions, and the internal capacity of the water tank is often limited, the hoses relying instead on fixed hydrants that restrict the operational responses of the riot-control team. Furthermore, by using such vehicles the military or law enforcement controllers can tarnish the reputation of the emergency services with the general public.

A Police Service of Northern Ireland (PSNI) Land Rover Tangi, 2013. Based on the Land Rover Defender 110 chassis, it is heavily armoured to protect from fire bombs and minor explosive devices. It is known as the 'meat wagon' in Northern Ireland. (Press Association)

This point is made in the US Army's Field Manual 19-15, *Civil Disturbances*, published in 1985:

> When using water, a number of factors must be considered. The Army does not have a water-dispersing system that is specifically designed for use in civil disturbance operations. Such a system can be improvised from existing equipment. The use of a large water tank – 750 to 1,000 gallons – and a powerful water pump mounted on a truck with a high-pressure hose and a nozzle capable of searching and traversing enables troops to employ water as they advance. By having at least two such water trucks, one can be kept in reserve.
>
> Employing water as a high-trajectory weapon, like rainfall, is highly effective during cold weather. When using water, as with other measures of force, certain restraints must be applied. Troops try to avoid using water on innocent bystanders like women and children. When water is used, the troops must provide the crowd with escape routes. Troops employing water must be protected by formations and, in some instances, by shields. The more severe use of water, the flat trajectory application, is employed only when necessary. Because fire departments are associated with saving lives and property rather than maintaining law and order, *fire department equipment must not be used for crowd control and dispersal.*
>
> – FM 19-15: 1985

This passage is interesting because it touches on the fact that RCVs are frequently by nature improvised vehicles, trucks simply adapted to carry water-jet equipment or other weapon options. But we also sense a clear hesitancy about using water as a riot-control measure. The 1960s news reels of civil-rights protesters being blasted by fire hoses left an indelible impression of US society, so much so that water-cannon technology or vehicles have rarely been used in riot contexts in the United States over the last four decades, and there are no signs of them coming back into fashion.

Military Armoured Vehicles as RCVs

During the politically and socially tumultuous Cold War, it frequently fell to the armed forces of many countries to quash or control civil disturbances. For this reason, armoured vehicles from military inventories were frequently pressed into the role of RCVs. Typically, the vehicles of choice were armoured cars and APCs. Popular choices included the BRDM amphibious scout car (in the Soviet Bloc), the M8 Greyhound armoured car (United States), Daimler Ferret (Britain), ENGESA EE-3 Jaraca Scout Car (Brazil) and the Fahd APC (Egypt). For riot duties specifically, such vehicles offer a blended spectrum of advantages and disadvantages. An obvious advantage is that they are tough, and designed to survive battlefield conditions. Their armour, which can often withstand small arms and cannon rounds, is therefore largely impervious to rioters' regular missiles of choice (although Molotov cocktails can still present a problem if accurately dropped onto an engine housing). Integral nuclear, biological and chemical (NBC) suites in some vehicles mean that they can also withstand the smoke and tear gas generated during riot conditions. Furthermore, purely military vehicles carry with them an undeniable intimidation factor; simply the presence of a brutal-looking armed vehicle can be enough to dissuade a crowd from aggressive action, although by the same token it can also inspire the crowd to a more panicked and dangerous response.

Using military-spec armoured vehicles as RCVs is not always a judicious choice. As the Tiananmen Square incident in 1989 demonstrated, determined rioters can stand up to the most bullish of vehicles (even a main battle tank), and modern thinking suggests that military vehicles actually heighten the perceived threat amongst crowds, and therefore precipitate rather than contain violence. Military vehicles often suffer from having fewer benign response options. A turreted 20mm or 30mm cannon might be ideal when engaging enemy armour on an open battlefield, but use it against rioters and human targets and the political fallout is likely to be grievous. Therefore, military vehicles purposed as RCVs tend to be used as secure platforms for ferrying riot-control troops to strategic key points, the main weaponry being either disengaged completely or left active as an option of last resort.

EXPLORING VARIANTS – BRITISH RCVs IN NORTHERN IRELAND

The period from the 1960s to the 1990s saw an increasing awareness of the particular requirements of RCVs, as opposed to other vehicles. One trend was the recognition that riot control needed a spectrum of RCV types, not just a single vehicle. While a heavier armoured car or water cannon might provide the forcible end of power projection, having smaller, more mobile, but still protected vehicles was a practical way of handling other riot-control tasks, such as reconnaissance and surveillance. One of the best ways to prise open this topic is to look at the RCVs used by the British in Northern Ireland during these decades.

The sheer frequency of riots and civil disturbances, plus the threat of outright military-level ambushes, produced a fascinating spectrum of RCVs in the troubled British territory. A photograph from Northern Ireland from the 1960s, below, shows the opposite extremes of British vehicular policing in the province. In the background is a crudely armoured JCB digger, the driver sitting in what looks akin to a steel sentry box. Lights and indicators on the sides are shielded by wire grills, to prevent their being smashed by missiles. Vehicles such as these were used to clear both the barricades and the debris of riots, shunting them aside with their powerful dozer blades. Despite (of because of) their basic armour, however, they remained vulnerable to the ingenuity of the rioters, hence they needed force protection. Such is provided in the foreground of this picture by an Alvis FV601 Saladin armoured car. This vehicle was actually developed in the immediate post-war period as a replacement for Daimler Mk II and AEC Mk II armoured cars. A fully turreted vehicle with a three-man crew, in its original format it was fitted with a 2-pdr cannon, but in the early 1950s this was upgraded to a higher-velocity 76mm L5A1 gun, capable of firing a variety of ammunition types from canister and high-explosive through to smoke and illumination. Sitting alongside the main gun was a coaxial 7.62mm machine gun. The Saladin was powered by a Rolls-Royce B80 Mk 6A eight-cylinder petrol engine developing 170bhp delivered to a six-wheel drive. These six wheels gave it a vertical obstacle capability of 0.46m and a trench-crossing capability of 1.52m, while maximum road speed was 72km/h. Armour was of a homogenous steel type, with a maximum depth of 32mm on the hull front and 16mm on the hull sides. Some were modified with extra armour for use in Northern Ireland, a response to the power of the improvised explosive devices (IEDs) utilized by Republican dissident forces. Further protection for the occupants was given by the engine

The Saladin armoured car was the more muscular face of riot-control duties and patrolling in Northern Ireland. Here it accompanies a crudely armoured digger, used to clear street barricades, burning cars and other obstacles. (Press Association)

An interior view of the Humber Pig. In total, eight people could occupy the rear cabin of the Pig, depending on the configuration of equipment inside. (Geni)

compartment's separation from the crew compartment by a fireproof bulkhead, plus an internal fire-extinguishing system.

The Saladin was a useful vehicle to deploy on very dangerous streets. It had speed, mobility and resilience, but apart from its grenade launchers – which could be used to dispense CS grenades and smoke during riots – its firepower was rather excessive for a civilian environment. (The cannon of the Saladin seen in the picture has its muzzle covered to tone down its threat, although this would not have stopped the gun being brought into action if necessary.)

Another vehicle of Alvis' FV600 series, and one that would become a near-iconic figure on the streets of Northern Ireland, was the FV603 Saracen APC. The prototype of the Saracen was produced in 1952, with production beginning the same year. It has many recognizable series features – the six-wheel drive configuration, an all-welded steel hull, the Rolls-Royce B-series engine and power-assisted steering on the front and centre road wheels – but with a personnel compartment set behind the driver's compartment, for eight soldiers to sit in two rows of inward-facing seats. Three shuttered apertures on either side of the crew compartment provide the occupants with visibility and firing ports when required, while the driver and commander at the front also both have hatched openings. The Saracen could be either turreted (mounting a Browning .30-cal machine gun) or without a turret. The latter configuration was more common in Northern Ireland, although a ring mount at the rear, on the roof of the crew compartment, could be fitted with a 7.62mm GPMG machine gun. Above each mudguard were three smoke-grenade launchers.

The Saracen was a hardy animal, tough enough to survive the riot conditions that prevailed almost nightly, while also providing protection against threats, either from a detonating roadside bomb or a burst from an AK-47. Nevertheless, such were the levels of danger from explosive devices and even some heavier weaponry (such as .50-cal sniper rifles) that during the 1970s and 1980s

1. MK 2 HUMBER PIG

A Humber Pig in classic green British Army colour scheme and configured as seen in Northern Ireland during the 1960s–80s. Specific riot-control features include the wide bull bars fitted to the front of the vehicle, plus a multi-directional gas-grenade launcher on the roof, which could scatter CS gas canisters over a wide area should the vehicle come under threat. (The specific grenade type was the Grenade Anti-Riot L11A1, each of which contained 23 CS pellets.) The overall bodywork is more heavily armoured than the initial Mk 1 variant, particularly around the doors and the sides of the rear cabin. The standard Mk 1 also had side storage boxes running around the rear wheel arch, but these were removed to prevent rioters placing explosive devices in them.

2. CZECH OKV-P

The Czech OKV-P is a variant of the Soviet-era BRDM-2 amphibious armoured scout car, which enjoyed huge export sales, serving with at least 38 different countries. The Czech vehicle is stripped of all the military versions' main weaponry, its main defensive options being its heavy armour, speed (up to 100km/h on the road) and gas grenades, launched from dispensers or from hand-held weapons by the riot squad in the back. A distinctive feature of the OKV-P is the option for fittings on the front hull. The two main options are a straightforward angled dozer blade and an extendible wire screen, to provide both shelter for riot troops and a broad shield to push back crowds.

1

2

POLICIE

A convoy of Saracen APCs patrols the streets of Northern Ireland in 1972. Attaching bull bars to the front of the vehicle converted it into a form of RCV, although its countermeasures (a 7.62mm machine gun) were generally not appropriate for civil disturbances. (Press Association)

armour plate was often welded directly onto the bodywork for additional protection. In the process, many up-armoured vehicles lost lateral stability, becoming top-heavy and requiring careful handling around sharp corners.

Another signature vehicle of the British days in Northern Ireland was the Humber Pig, utilized by the Royal Ulster Constabulary (RUC) as well as the British Army. (The RUC Pigs could be distinguished by their grey colour scheme, as opposed to the Army green.) The Pig – so called after its squat and inelegant appearance – was a four-wheel-drive vehicle created in the 1950s by adding an armoured shell to a 1-ton Humber truck. They were actually not intended for long-term use – rather as expedient armoured vehicles while other specific vehicle types were being developed. Yet as the Troubles in Northern Ireland grew more bitter and lethal, the Pigs were pressed into service once again.

The main version in operation in Northern Ireland was the Mk 2, which was essentially a Mk 1 but up-armoured to protect against IEDs, heavy-calibre bullets and RPG anti-tank weapons. They also received heavy bull bars at the front, designed to shunt aside barricades and other street-straddling obstacles, and a heavy tailboard to protect the feet of soldiers disembarking or who were standing behind the vehicle. The side stowage boxes that featured on the Mk 1 vehicles were removed, as these would act as traps for incendiary devices or as places in which booby traps might be placed. Thus modified, the Pig weighed 7.5 tonnes, embodied in dimensions of 4.93m long, 2.04m wide and 2.12m high. In addition to the two-man crew, the vehicle could carry eight passengers. Power came from a Rolls-Royce B60 six-cylinder 4.2-litre petrol engine, giving a top speed of 64km/h.

The Pig was also field modified for various purposes, each version attracting a different adjective as follows:

- Flying Pig – This was a standard Mk 2 but fitted with extending riot screens on either side of the cabin; these could be folded out to provide a protective wall for troops and police.
- Holy Pig – With a passing resemblance to a church pulpit (hence its name) the 'Holy Pig' featured a rooftop hatch surrounded by a perspex screen, providing protection for an observer during civil disturbances.
- Kremlin Pig – This variant featured extensive wire screening around the body to protect against the RPG-7 rocket-propelled grenade. The wire cage was designed to initiate detonation of the shaped-charge warhead before it struck the main body of the vehicle, weakening its penetrative power.
- Squirt Pig – Appropriately named, the Squirt Pig was fitted with a water cannon beside the driver, to hose down protesters. Water tanks were fitted into the rear compartment.
- Foaming Pig – This vehicle was fitted with a foam generator, used to dispense blast-and-fire-suppressive foam around IEDs.
- Felix Pig – The Felix Pig was modified for use by explosive ordnance disposal (EOD) teams, holding all their equipment and communications systems.

An Alvis Saracen sits outside a house in Londonderry in 1972, waiting for trouble. This is a turreted version, fitted with a 7.62mm machine gun. Note the extensive barricade ram at the front and the wire mesh covering the headlamps. (Press Association)

- Turreted Pig – This version of the Pig was less of an RCV and more of an armoured car. It featured the machine-gun-armed turret of the Shorland Armoured Car (see below), and was used to patrol the dangerous Armagh borderlands.

The Pig became, much like the Saracen, a virtual symbol of the Troubles in Northern Ireland. Yet equal status was held by the varieties of military and RUC armoured Land Rovers in the province.

Introduced into service in 1965, the Shorland armoured patrol car was operated by the RUC, although from 1970 it was transferred to the Ulster Defence Force (UDF), a transition that saw the grey police vehicles repainted in a militaristic green. The vehicle, despite its extensive modifications, was still recognizably part of the Land Rover stable – it was built upon a 109in. wheelbase Series Two Land Rover chassis. The Shorland took the chassis and topped it with a heavily armoured body fitted with shuttered windows. (The armour was 7.25mm thick with a Brinnel Hardness of 363.) On top of the basic crew compartment was the turret of a Ferret armoured car, equipped with either a 7.62mm machine gun or gas-grenade dispensers. Coping with the extra weight placed upon the chassis was, initially, a 67bhp engine, but in subsequent marks the powerplant was upgraded. The 1972 Mk 3, for example, had a 91bhp engine, although the extra power was offset by increased armour. In 1980 the Mk 4 began production, this time with a powerful 3.5-litre Rover V8 engine (which necessitated moving the radiator further forward) and improved armour. The Mk 4 also had air conditioning fitted as standard, plus air-extractor systems, both welcome additions for those who had to spend much time within the vehicles.

The finale of the Shorland is the Series 5, which used the Defender 110 chassis to create an entire series of military vehicles, the purpose of each vehicle varying on the internal and external fittings. The main versions of the series used for RCV duties are the S51 and S52 Armoured Patrol Cars, the latter being the eventual replacement for the former. The S51 and S52 are powered by 3.5-litre Rover V8 petrol engines or 2.5-litre Rover Tdi turbodiesel engines. The turret is gone, an acknowledgement of the over-militarized appearance, but the armour is of superior quality to the preceding vehicles. Compared with the S51, the S52 has a larger cabin area and also an enlarged escape hatch at the rear, in case the vehicle has to be abandoned in haste. Extra fitment on the vehicles includes (courtesy of the Shorts concern) smoke-grenade dischargers, air conditioning, run-flat tyres, a PA system, bullet-resistant glass windscreens, multiple firing/vision ports, a heater/demister and fire-extinguisher system.

The inventory of Shorland Land Rover vehicles is complicated by the addition of the Shorts Armoured Personnel Vehicle (APV) series, which on first glance appear largely to be Shorland cars minus the turret. The first of the vehicles was the Shorland SB301, the 'SB' standing for Shorts Brothers, who produced the vehicle as a private venture based on the Shorland Mk 3. It could carry a total crew of eight people, but it had no active ventilation system – if the occupants wanted fresh air, they simply had to open some or all of the eight gun ports and the hatches over the front doors. The SB301 was supplemented in 1986 by the SB401, based on the Shorland Mk 4, with the extractor fan as standard plus numerous fitment options, such as vision blocks instead of pistol ports.

The Shorts/Shorland interaction continued in the Series 5 vehicles, especially in the S55 Armoured Personnel Carrier. The S55, using the Defender 110 chassis, provided a more comfortable operating experience for the occupants by lowering the cross-country maximum speed (from 48km/h to 40km/h). Its RCV survivability was also improved. Whereas early S55s had visor protection and door hatches over the windows, later versions replaced these features with armoured glass and armoured vision ports fitted above each gun port. The bull bar at the front could be hinged forward to provide protection from rolled threats (such as beer barrels) and also to make obstacle clearance more effective. Guttering around the doors gave a controlled flow route for burning fluids to drain away from the vehicle; this feature is seen on most Shorland vehicles.

Our examination of the Shorland/Shorts vehicles is not the end of our study of the RCV Land Rovers in Northern Ireland. The intensity of the conflict meant that existing RUC, UDF and British Army fleets of Land Rovers had to be adapted to the conditions with urgency and realism. For the British Army, the solution to protecting its fleet of 88in. and 109in. Land Rovers came in the form of the Vehicle Protection Kit (VPK), which was essentially a system of bolt-on glass-reinforced plastic (GRP) armour pieces. Clear Makrolon sheets were fitted to windscreens and door windows to provide impact resistance over

A Humber Pig advances down the Falls Road in Belfast, 1977. It has extended riot screens on either side of the hull; these formed a useful protective shield for officers and soldiers during riot conditions, as well as increasing the vehicle's ability to push back crowds. (Press Association)

those vulnerable points, while GRP sheets shielded bodywork.

The VPK was introduced in the 1970s, and it took up to 35 man-hours to fit a single kit to a Land Rover. While the kit certainly improved the protection for the crew, it did little to enhance the performance of the vehicle, which became rather top-heavy. Nevertheless, the concept was proven, and in the mid-1980s an improved HV VPK was introduced (often referred to as the 'Piglet'), just prior to the Army's introduction of the Land Rover 110 Armoured Patrol Vehicle. The 'HV' of the title referred to 'High Velocity', and indicated that the protection kit was intended to withstand high-velocity small-arms rounds. The extra weight required to provide this protection was substantial – in total the modified vehicle weighed 2.5 tonnes. Indeed, amongst the fitting instructions provided with the kit was: 'Note, to refit door the vehicle must be standing on its road wheels and not on jacks or axle stands, this minimises chassis bend.'

The Mk 1 Shorland armoured car. This is the original 'boat tail' Shorland, which had a crew capacity of just three people. Later versions extended the personnel capacity to eight people (two crew up-front plus six in the rear). (Geni)

The VPK Land Rovers were just some of the Land Rover modifications for riot and security use in Northern Ireland. The RUC, for example, developed the Hotspur Land Rover, a Land Rover 109 with an internal armoured steel second roof plus other ballistic protection fitted to body panels. Rubber and metal grilles around the skirts prevented objects being thrown under the vehicle, and in the early 1980s Hotspurs were also fitted with a passenger-operated fire-extinguisher system. The RUC in the 1980s used, in limited numbers, the Land Rover Simba, this being purpose-designed for riot duties, with 360-degree protection supplied via a complete armoured shell. The Land Rover Tangi, based on the Defender 110 chassis, improved matters significantly. Not only did the vehicle enjoy the comforts of the Defender series, including air conditioning and power steering, but it also had some intelligent protective additions, such as a fire-retardant fabric strip around the bonnet edge and at the hinge between the bonnet and the front bulkhead, plus enhanced protection over the radiator. The vehicle was later fitted with the 'Dawson Roof', a double-layer armoured roof designed to defeat shaped-charge 'drogue' bombs. These vehicles are still running on the streets of Northern Ireland today.

The front line for RCVs. Riot police in Tangi Land Rovers, backed by a water-cannon vehicle, deal with a disturbance in the Ardoyne area of Belfast, 2011. Water cannon are also useful for extinguishing street fires in places too dangerous for the regular fire brigade. (Sineakee)

International Developments

The case study of Northern Ireland provides us with a useful snapshot of the nature of RCVs during the 1970s, 1980s and into the 1990s. We see a mixed package – straight-up military APCs and armoured cars, hastily adapted light vehicles and more purpose-designed

The South African Casspir, despite its historically poor public relations, remains an excellent APC and RCV. Here we see the vehicle standing guard over a shopping mall in South Africa in 2010. (Warrenski)

armoured vehicles. The arsenal of vehicles also included, from the 1960s, the German-made Mayer water cannon mentioned previously.

Looking beyond Britain, we see an extremely varied picture. Some countries, particularly in the developing world, controlled riots with whatever was to hand – heavily armoured vehicles on the one hand, crudely up-armoured light vehicles on the other. Some nations, however, reflect the Northern Ireland experience more accurately, having invested specifically in vehicles designed to handle near-constant internal conflict.

The natural place to go for this study is South Africa, which during the apartheid era experienced riots on a prodigious scale of regularity and violence. Of all the vehicles used by the South African Police to quell the riots, the Casspir was the most iconic and notorious. The Casspir was in essence a military design, an infantry mobility vehicle developed during the 1970s by the Council for Scientific and Industrial Research (CSIR) as a versatile combat platform for South African police and security forces. Central to the Casspir's design was the V-shaped armoured monocoque hull. This was designed specifically to survive landmine or IED detonations by deflecting the blast outwards and away from the crew compartment. (It was originally produced in response to South African forces' experience in the border wars, where landmine attacks against vehicles were common.) To give the vehicle exceptional mobility, the wheelbase was set high (360mm at the rear), lifting up a capacious ten-man rear cabin with central, outward-facing seating and vision/firing ports along the side. Entry to the cabin was via a large rear door, but roof hatches were also provided – these were useful for police to conduct riot observation from a high vantage point.

The major versions of the Casspir during the 1980s and 1990s were the Mk I and Mk II, which shared the same basic technical specifications. The one-piece hull was of blast-protected armoured steel fitted with tough polycarbonate laminated glass, resilient to small-arms fire of up to 7.62mm calibre. The vehicle could survive the detonation of up to three 7kg blast landmines beneath the hull. Overall dimensions were 6.9m long, 3.125m high and 2.45m wide. The powerplant was the 6-litre ADE 352T direct-injection turbocharged diesel, allied to a five-speed gearbox.

The real strength of the Casspir was not only its resilience to damage and its mobility, but also its flexibility as a platform. It was adapted into more than ten configurations, including a dedicated RCV, which featured larger windows along the cabin side to improve crew visibility in riot conditions. Its evolution has also continued. The latest Mk IV version, produced by Mechem Vehicles, has improved belly protection (up to 21kg of TNT under a wheel) plus an enhanced 6.7-litre Cummins powerplant that generates 205kW of output, as opposed to the 124kW of the Mk II. The one problem with the Casspir, however, is that its role in suppressing anti-apartheid riots gave it an image problem, not helped by its 'aggressive' military appearance. For this reason, the South African Police Service auctioned off their stock of Casspirs in 2008. However, as far back as 1987 the South African authorities were replacing some Casspirs with a less-martial-looking vehicle. The RCV 9 Nonqai –

the name is a Zulu word for 'protector' or 'peacemaker' – looks more like a muscular four-wheel-drive camper van, albeit one equipped with a welded all-steel armour body, bulletproof windows (plus protective grilles), a pneumatically controlled barricade bumper and run-flat tyres.

In post-Soviet Russia, the authorities still have an entire generation of Red Army armoured vehicles to assist with their riot control, but the security forces also invested in more specialist vehicles, particularly water cannon. During the early 1990s, the secretive and notorious OMON internal security force developed a new vehicle for its civil-disturbance inventory – the Lavina (Avalanche). The foundation of the vehicle was the 8x8 chassis of the BAZ-69501 truck, powered by two Kamaz 740 V8 engines. To this chassis was mounted a heavily armoured cabin for four crew members, the cabin featuring bulletproof glass and protective grilles, plus a 10,000-litre water storage tank feeding two independently rotatable water-jet nozzles above the cabin. (A shorter version of the vehicle was also created, with an 8,000-litre tank.) The Avalanche was partly intended for fire-fighting duties, but also offered a formidable riot-control presence when required; in this capacity optional equipment included a loudspeaker system for addressing recalcitrant crowds and an emergency fire-extinguishing system.

Yet the Avalanche was really transformed in the Avalanche-M variant. The front bumper received an obstacle-clearance blade, and the vehicle sides were mounted with grenade launchers for firing tear gas or rubber bullets. The rear of the vehicle was fitted with a smoke-generating system, while the loudspeaker system was uprated to the 500-watt SSU-500. The latest version of the Avalanche, introduced into the Moscow police in 2004, is the Lavina-Uragan (Avalanche-Hurricane), built on the chassis of a Ural-532 362. The Hurricane was designed to be more compact than the massive preceding models, and easier to maintain, plus its cabin benefits from the computerization of controls that has characterized RCV design over the last 20 years.

Looking around the rest of the world, we also find certain manufacturers becoming dominant and productive players in the manufacture of RCVs. A case in point is Beit Alpha Technologies (BAT) in Israel, which has been in the business of producing specialist security vehicles since 1966. Its inventory of RCVs, ageing and modern, now runs to more than 15 vehicles. The core platforms include a GM Sierra, GM Silverado, Chevrolet CC5500,

The Lavina-Uragan (Avalanche-Hurricane) is used by the Moscow OMON security forces, plus other law enforcement agencies in Russia and the former Soviet Union. It is based around a Ural-532362 chassis. (Vitaly Kuzmin)

The ABS-40 Lavina RCV is a powerful water-cannon system built upon a BAZ-6953 chassis. The vehicle is mounted with two independently directable water jets, controlled from inside the armoured cab. (Vitaly Kuzmin)

MB Unimog and KAMAZ. Fittings to these vehicles, as listed on the company's website, illustrate the sophistication that RCVs have reached in their offensive and defensive options:

- Three different modes of firing water cannon: short pulse, long pulse and continuous stream.
- Tear gas (CS) or pepper spray (OC) mixed into the water.
- Dye colouring mixed into the water.
- Under-chassis and upper-deck foam protection (against firebombs).
- Tear-gas nozzles for all-round protection of the vehicle.
- Water sprayers for windshield and side windows.
- Air filtration for driver's cabin.

B

1. OMON LAVINA-URAGAN WATER-CANNON VEHICLE

The Lavina-Uragan (Avalanche-Hurricane) is built on the 8x8 chassis of the Ural-532362, and is the most modern addition to the Lavina line of water-cannon vehicles. The water tank holds 9,000 litres with a JAMZ-236 engine providing power for the water jet, delivered to the cab-mounted nozzles. Miniature surveillance cameras are mounted onto the body at key points, these feeding through to monitors inside the cab and a VCR unit to record all the external footage. A 500-watt speaker system is also installed over the cab. The hydraulically powered blade in front of the cab is raised for road travel and lowered for obstacle clearance. The vehicle we see here is painted in the livery of the Moscow OMON, a controversial paramilitary police force that was founded in 1979 on SWAT-type principles.

2. ALVIS OMC CASSPIR

Here we see an apartheid-era police Casspir. The view clearly shows the angled lower hull of the vehicle. Not only does this provide partial deflection of under-belly explosions, it also makes the job of climbing up onto the vehicle more problematic for aggressors. As a police version of the Casspir, the side windows are larger than the military APC. Note also the firing ports beneath the windows, six on each side. The police officers inside could also gain a high vantage point through the roof hatches. The total weight of the Casspir was 10.88 tonnes, and to power such a hefty vehicle it was fitted with an Atlantis Diesel Engines OM352A turbocharged diesel engine, generating 124kW of power. Note that the name 'Casspir' is an anagram of the vehicle's designers: the South African Police (SAP) and the Council for Scientific and Industrial Research (CSIR).

1

МИЛИЦИЯ
МОСКВА
ГУВД
ОМОН

2

- Front bulldozer for obstacle removal.
- Closed-circuit TV and video system.
- Rear camera and monitor for rearwards visibility.
- Ballistic armouring against any threat level.
- Run-flat tyres
- Front bumper water/foam monitor.

Note how many of these features emphasize operator comfort and 360-degree surveillance. One of the shifts in RCV design from the late 20th century was that designers gave more consideration to crew comfort and operability. Computerized control systems were key to this, with all-round cameras giving the operators the reassurance of 360-degree surveillance plus the ability to identify, track and target individuals far more accurately.

Some manufacturers sought to produce complete RCV packages in a single unit. A notable example of such a vehicle, brought to public attention by its featuring on the BBC's *Top Gear* programme, is the Locomotors Talon. Only nine of these British vehicles were produced, in the 1980s and 1990s. The core is based on a 4x4 Bedford truck chassis. Powered by an 8.2-litre turbodiesel (top speed was about 100km/h and fuel economy was a costly 6mpg), the Talon had a two-man crew plus seating for 12 more in the back. As is standard for modern RCVs, the Talon had a heavily armoured body, but also the interesting addition of an outer skin that could be electrified if need be, to prevent people climbing on it. If paint was thrown over the windows, solvent window washers would soon clear the screen. Offensive fittings included a single turreted water cannon, set over the driver cab, plus a total of 16 grenade launchers. The vehicle was also fitted with a sonorous PA system and extendible floodlighting. But what made the Talon notable was its self-sufficiency. On-board equipment included a fridge and a chemical toilet, and its extensive surveillance and communications systems meant that it could act as a hub for riot operations across a wide urban area. As history turned out, the Talon found no use in the UK security or military services, and the existing vehicles went into the hands of foreign governments and private collectors.

The evolution of the RCV from 1945 to the 2000s, as the narrative above explores, has been a mix of improvised design response and, at the same time, an awareness that RCVs need a unique set of properties that have to be reflected in the vehicles' configuration. This picture remains as we bring the story up to the present day, but we also see the appearance of RCVs that offer more precise extensions of power on disrupted streets.

The driver's position in the Paramount Group Maverick. The driver can centrally control the tyre pressure, lower/raise the pneumatic dozer blade and bullbars and also monitor the rear of the vehicle via cameras linked to internal monitors. (Paramount Group)

MODERN VARIANTS – STATE OF THE ART

The RCVs emerging from the world's key manufacturers in the 2000s could not be more different from the improvised or crudely designed versions that policed riots in the 1940s and 1950s. Not only have they benefited from the latest advances in material technology, but computerization has also revolutionized the way that they can be operated. Now

Under test conditions, a Paramount Maverick makes a steep ascent. Excellent mobility was a central objective of the Maverick's design; it can tackle gradients of up to 60 degrees head on, and cross laterally slopes of 35 degrees. (Paramount Group)

a single individual, ensconced in his heavily armoured cab, can control multiple responses to the riot, while remaining fully aware of the tactical situation through 360-degree surveillance plus integration into a tactical web. The large variety of such vehicles available on today's market means that we can only study a select few in depth here, but they are representative of the types.

South Africa has continued its strong tradition of producing resilient and format-flexible RCVs, particularly in excellent vehicles such as the Paramount company's Maverick. In overall layout it has a rather unthreatening bus-like appearance – the low-key visual impact is part of a deliberate design strategy to reduce levels of perceived threat amongst volatile crowds. This being said, the Maverick is open to being fitted with lethal weapon systems when required. Options cited by the company's literature include 7.62mm machine guns on pintle mounts through to electrically driven turrets mounting 12.7mm and 14.5mm machine guns, and even 40mm grenade launchers. With such fitment, the vehicle essentially becomes an IFV.

The INKAS Armored Riot Control Vehicle, made by INKAS® Armored Vehicle Manufacturing, certainly projects power. Built on a Freightliner M2106 RCV chassis, it has a 10,000-litre water tank, with water delivery speeds of 1,900 litres per minute. (INKAS)

This cutaway of the Paramount Group Maverick Internal Security Vehicle (ISV) shows the vehicle in the manufacturer's generic livery, before delivery and customization to clients. The overall arrangement features the driver and co-driver up-front in a protected cab, while in the main passenger compartment there is seating for up to 12 people, depending on the variable configuration of the seating layout. Just behind the driver seat is a computer station for monitoring surveillance from the vehicle's external cameras. The floor of the vehicle provides ballistic protection from light explosive devices, up to an M26 hand grenade in power, while the bodywork and windows can resist 7.62x54mm armour-piercing rounds, even those fired at relatively close ranges. Options for fitment include fire-suppression systems, wire-cutter attachments, vehicle/personnel tracking system, weapon stations and turrets and public address system.

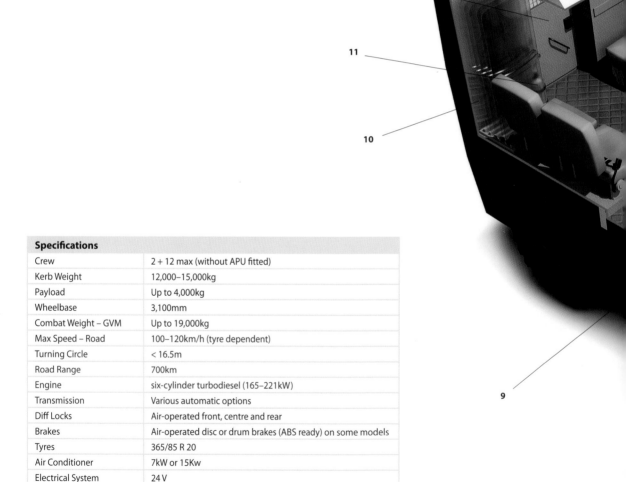

Specifications	
Crew	2 + 12 max (without APU fitted)
Kerb Weight	12,000–15,000kg
Payload	Up to 4,000kg
Wheelbase	3,100mm
Combat Weight – GVM	Up to 19,000kg
Max Speed – Road	100–120km/h (tyre dependent)
Turning Circle	< 16.5m
Road Range	700km
Engine	six-cylinder turbodiesel (165–221kW)
Transmission	Various automatic options
Diff Locks	Air-operated front, centre and rear
Brakes	Air-operated disc or drum brakes (ABS ready) on some models
Tyres	365/85 R 20
Air Conditioner	7kW or 15Kw
Electrical System	24 V
KE Protection	(Standard): Up to STANAG 4569 level 3
Blast Protection	M26 hand grenade protection

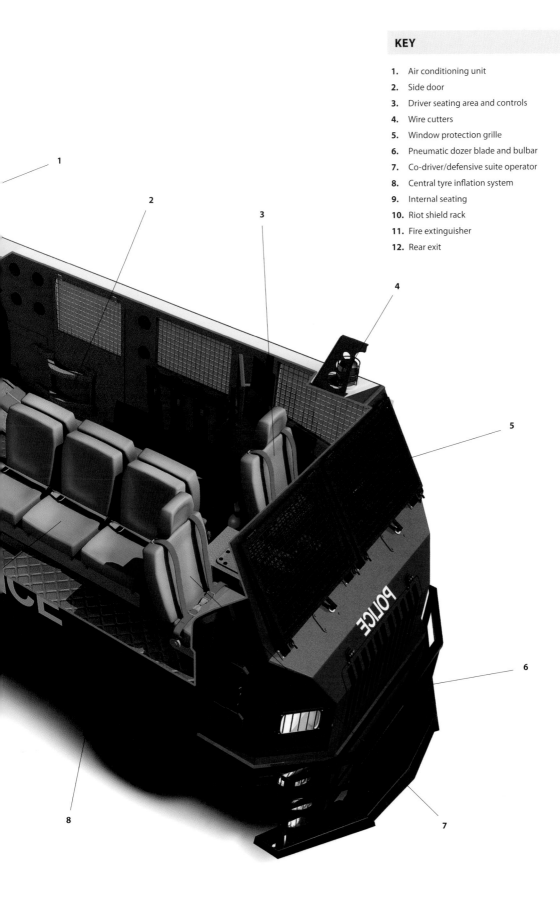

KEY

1. Air conditioning unit
2. Side door
3. Driver seating area and controls
4. Wire cutters
5. Window protection grille
6. Pneumatic dozer blade and bulbar
7. Co-driver/defensive suite operator
8. Central tyre inflation system
9. Internal seating
10. Riot shield rack
11. Fire extinguisher
12. Rear exit

The forward cab of the Paramount Maverick. Note how the windows are covered with wire mesh. Although the windows themselves are bulletproof, the mesh protects them further from thrown and hand-held weapon impacts, and helps to maintain occupant visibility. (Paramount Group)

In overall outline the Maverick measures 6m long, 2.7m wide and 2.9m high, and the core vehicle provides the platform for various adaptations, including police internal security vehicle (ISV), SWAT APC, rapid intervention water cannon (RICW), mobile adjustable ramp system (MARS) and explosive ordnance disposal (EOD) vehicle. Whatever the configuration, however, the vehicle has substantial levels of physical protection built into its structure. The body and armoured glass have ballistic protection for small-arms rounds up to 7.62x51mm. Furthermore, armoured belly plates can be fitted beneath the vehicle to protect the occupants from grenades or small IEDs exploding directly below. Fire prevention comes in the form of manual and automatic extinguishing systems fitted at key points, such as the wheel arches. To protect and enhance its mobility, the vehicle has run-flat inserts in the tyres plus a central tyre inflation system (CTIS), so that the ground pressure of the tyres can be adjusted according to the terrain. The vehicle can cross a 6m ditch, climb a 3.5m-high obstacle and ascend a 60-degree gradient, plus ford up to 4m of water without preparation. Multiple CCTV cameras provide the vehicle operators with excellent situational awareness.

Looking at the variants of the Maverick, the key types for RCV duties are the police ISV and the RIWC. The former can be fitted with external riot-control equipment, such as dozer blade, bull bar and grenade launchers. Internally, the seating is configured to hold two operators (in the forward cab) plus up to 12 fully equipped response officers, along with all their riot gear stored ready for use. Front and central side doors, plus a large rear door, means that the occupants can enter and exit rapidly.

The RIWC is, according to company publicity, 'specifically suited for the control of small crowds, to prevent the formation of large crowds and to complement larger water cannon vehicles by controlling and managing the movement of persons on the flanks of large crowds. The vehicle is also particularly suitable for operations to "snatch" riot leaders and organisers by isolating them from the crowd.' The RIWC is essentially the Maverick fitted

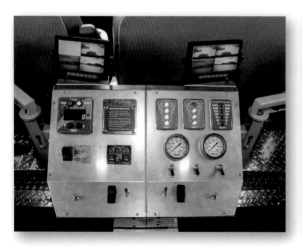

Another view of the INKAS Armored Riot Control Vehicle. Wire-mesh protection is provided on all windows, and the bodywork has ballistic protection up to 7.62x54mm/.308 Winchester. Door and window apertures are overlapped to avoid presenting crowbar-friendly attack points. (INKAS)

with a 4,500-litre water tank, the contents of which can be dispensed at 1,500 litres a minute through a top-mounted water jet. Power for the water cannon comes from an independent diesel engine, and total range for the jet is 70m. In an interesting protective addition, the RIWC also features a rear-mounted water jet, to blast away those enterprising individuals who feel motivated to climb on the rear of the vehicle.

The Maverick is a tough, mobile and powerful RCV, one of a new breed. Competitors to the Maverick include the Canadian company INKAS, who currently offer muscular options such as the Armored Riot Control Vehicle. This rather menacing-looking water-cannon unit is built upon a Freightliner M2106 RCV chassis, and is powered by a Cummins ISC300 diesel engine. It is heavily armoured against small-arms fire and grenade-level explosive threats, with the armour protection wrapping around the engine bay, fuel tank and air brake cylinders as well as the crew cabin. A no-nonsense height-adjustable bumper on the front delivers effective obstacle clearance. The business of crowd clearance is conducted by a turret-mounted water jet, drawing on a 10,000-litre stainless steel water tank, and with 320-degrees of rotation. Like the Maverick, the water jet can be set to pulse delivery, the pulses being of between half a second and two-and-a-half seconds duration. The water tank also supplies a fire-suppression system, via a system of nozzles situated at strategic points around the vehicle.

Although RCVs have become increasingly sophisticated during their history, in many ways the core tools of riot control have stayed the same – water and gas, with the occasional rubber bullet or even lethal bullet thrown in as more aggressive options. However, a new generation of RCVs is starting to emerge that take threat control to even more persuasive levels. Most striking is the US military's Active Denial System (ADS). The ADS is in itself not a vehicle, but rather a non-lethal directed-energy weapon, looking rather like an airport radar dish. What the ADS does is fire a heat-ray, similar in principle to the energy emitted by a microwave oven. Those in the path of the ray experience a rapid warming of the skin, until it feels like an excruciating sunburn, caused by the ray exciting fat and water molecules in the skin's surface. Crowds disperse briskly when targeted by such a weapon, but once they are out of the path of the ray their skin sensations quickly return to normal.

OPPOSITE LEFT
The defensive foam operating system aboard the Paramount Maverick Rapid Intervention Water Cannon (RIWC). The foam creates a slick surface on roads and pavements, making it difficult for rioters to gain traction with their feet. (Paramount Group)

OPPOSITE RIGHT
Water and foam in the Paramount Maverick Rapid Intervention Water Cannon (RIWC) are controlled from a station just behind the driver's seat. Joystick controls, allied to external monitors, allow the operator to target the jet precisely, down to individual level. (Paramount)

Here we see the US military Active Denial System (ADS) mounted in two configurations, including a Humvee on the right. The major challenge for this system is ensuring that it is protected from missiles, as its array is vulnerable to attack. (DoD)

The ADS can be mounted on a variety of platforms, but the most popular is on the back of a specially adapted High Mobility Multipurpose Wheeled Vehicle (HMMWV) 'Humvee'. In itself, the Humvee is not an ideal RCV. It is intended more as a light infantry mobility vehicle rather than a frontline tool, although the wars in Iraq and Afghanistan have seen it thrust into combat roles on numerous occasions. Indeed, the controversy surrounding the Humvee's vulnerability in Iraq led, from 2004, to many of the vehicles being fitted with up-armour kits to protect against IEDs and land mines. Publicly available images of the Humvee ADS, however, show vehicles without the additional armour, likely because the extra plating would interfere with the free movement of the ADS dish. For this reason, their value as RCVs is open to question, although the potential of the weapon for dispersing crowds is apparent and apparently Israel is exploring the potential of a similar system called WaveStun.

Another vehicle-mounted technology being investigated by the world's military and police forces is generically known as the long-range acoustic

D

1. US ARMY ACTIVE DENIAL SYSTEM

The future of riot-control vehicles? This is the US military's Active Denial System (ADS), mounted on a Humvee light vehicle. In itself, the Humvee is not an ideal RCV, but the addition of the ADS unit gives it potentially powerful crowd-dispersal capabilities. The emitter, when activated, projects a 3.2mm-wavelength high-energy beam that causes an intense burning sensation on the skin, even if shielded by clothing. In tests, people were generally able to endure the beam for 3–5 seconds before having to flee the scene. The system is operated by a single individual within the Humvee's cab – the soldier simply places cross-hairs on the target (an individual or small group) via a monitor display, and pulls the trigger on a control joystick. Physical effects are felt as far as 550m away.

2. CHINESE ZFB05 PSYOPS

In contrast to the ADS, the Chinese ZFB05 Psyops vehicle is armed with little more than two roof-mounted speakers, plus gas grenade dispensers as more aggressive options. It is based on the standard ZFB05 APC chassis and body, manufactured by the Shaanxi Baoji Special Vehicles Manufacturing Company. To monitor crowds, a CCTV camera is mounted at the rear of the vehicle on a telescoping mount, which can be extend the camera to 6m above the ground. This versatile vehicle also boasts an NBC suite plus a night-vision driving system.

1

2

Polish police confront a crowd of protestors in Warsaw in 2011. The vehicle is a Mitsubishi L200 and is mounted with the LRAD-500 acoustic hailing device. As well as being used to broadcast messages, the system can deliver targeted and painful blasts of sound. (Adam Kliczek, http://zatrzymujeczas.pl)

device (LRAD). Essentially this is a loudspeaker system fitted to the roof of a vehicle that can deliver targeted bursts of sound at excruciating levels, sufficient to cause nausea and disorientation by affecting the inner ear. The LRAD can also be used to transmit simple messages, rather than pain. These systems are now seen internationally, from ESU units on the streets of New York, with police units in Poland and with Israeli Army psychological-warfare units in Palestine (here the device is appropriately known as 'The Scream'). The vehicular platforms for the LRAD can vary considerably, from light vehicles to APCs.

A picture is emerging. In one sense, the technical development of the RCV has reached a stable point, in terms of bodywork, mobility, armoured protection and communications. The current and future areas of investment are therefore likely to be in weapon systems. As well as new tools such as the ADS and LRAD, options being trialled or deployed around the world include paintball guns, 'skunk spray' (a liquid with a vomit-inducing stench) and bean-bag bullets, designed to inflict heavy bruising injuries but without penetration. In Israel, a development called the 'Thunder Blaster' is a device that emits huge and rapid explosions by igniting petroleum gas; anyone under 50m from the blasts will be either deafened or, according to some concerns, even killed by the roar.

Elsewhere, furthermore, security companies are now exploring the use of drones as RCVs, getting away from the dangers of putting personnel on the front line in the first place. The South African company Desert Wolf has produced a remotely controlled eight-bladed mini-helicopter known as 'The Skunk', equipped with four guns capable of firing paintballs, plastic bullets or pepper spray, plus a thermal camera, HD video camera and light-and-sound systems. Some purchases have already been made by mining companies. The future of riot control is now beginning its next generational leap.

OPERATIONAL HISTORY

It would be impossible here to describe in detail the use of RCVs in every historical context since the end of World War II. RCVs of every description have been deployed to literally tens of thousands of riots across the world by all manner of regimes. Their applications against citizenry have made them particularly controversial vehicles, often attracting the opprobrium of the press and public. Yet they have also undoubtedly saved the lives of hundreds of military personnel and police officers, thrust into the midst of some of the most intimidating situations imaginable. What we can do here is examine some key themes and moments in the history of RCVs, as well as giving analysis on their tactical opportunities and vulnerabilities.

The TAM 110 is a light RCV used by the Serbian Gendarmerie for riot control. The rear cage acts as both a protective shield for officers and an improvised holding cell for apprehended rioters. (Boris Dimitrov)

During the 1950s and 1960s there was a decidedly mixed picture of tactics and technology being deployed onto the streets. On the one hand, the application of military vehicles to riot-control duties was common in both the communist East and capitalist West. The reasons for this were largely that many nations had yet to develop specialist riot-control units, and so relied upon reserve or regular military units to deal with civil disturbances. In the Soviet Union, T-34/85 and T-54/55 main battle tanks were most conspicuously deployed to quash the Hungarian Revolution of 1956, and in the subsequent decade various configurations of the BRDM scout car gave service in policing troubled towns and cities in the Soviet Bloc. Similarly, in the United States the M8 Greyhound and (from 1960) M113 APCs appeared on the streets of US cities during the horrendous riots of the 1950s and 1960s, typically in the hands of National Guard units. The extent of the riots, however, also meant that many police departments felt the need to purchase armoured cars for their own riot-control duties, an option made easier by the huge amount of war surplus still on offer during these decades. A major turning point in this regard was the 1965 Watts Riots in Los Angeles, which ran from 11 to 17 August 1965. In what amounted to a six-day battle, 34 people were killed and 1,032 injured, despite thousands of police officers and National Guardsmen being deployed onto the streets. The conditions of the riot were later vividly described by an LAPD field commander:

> We had no idea how to deal with this. There were seventy of us, eight hundred of them, maybe a thousand as the night wore on. We were constantly ducking bottles, rocks, knives and Molotov cocktails. One officer was stabbed in the back. Guns were poked out of second-story windows, random shots fired. The rioters uprooted wooden bus-stop benches, pulling them out of their concrete bases and setting them on fire. Firemen couldn't get through – or wouldn't, terrified of being shot at. Two or three television mobile units were damaged, along with fifty to sixty vehicles. It was random chaos, in small disparate patches… Undermanned and overwhelmed, we responded cautiously. Guns were not to be used unless an officer clearly felt that his life was threatened.
> Gates: 1992, p.91

The chaos of the Watts Riots was not isolated. The Newark Riots in New Jersey and the Detroit Riots, both in July 1967, left 69 people dead, to name just two more of the riots that afflicted the United States during this time. In the soul-searching analysis that followed, two conclusions became clear: 1) The police needed better-coordinated responses to riot conditions, without necessarily requiring military support; 2) riot officers needed better

Modern riot units often deploy mixed types of vehicles to deter and disperse crowds. Here, in Hanover, Germany in 1995, police deploy a fast, light armoured vehicle for mobility, backed by the threat of a water cannon towering behind. (Press Association)

protection from the variety of riot threats. The latter conclusion led to many police departments purchasing and adapting armoured vehicles. For example, the LA and Detroit police forces both purchased M8 armoured cars and M113 APCs. Gates later defended the APC purchase by stating to reporters: 'I realize how valuable it would have been in Watts, where we had nothing to protect us from sniper fire when we tried to rescue wounded officers.'

In 1967, the US Army also began to review its riot-control tactics. Central to the tactical thinking was the presentation of overwhelming vehicular force. Military sources acquired by the *New York Times* stated that 'Tanks and armored personnel carriers provided shock action which may assist in deterring would-be rioters ... the use of pedestal-mounted machine guns on the patrol vehicles has a psychological as well as real advantage.' Interestingly the document states that the first line in riot control is the presentation of 'armed troops in formation with vehicles in full view of the mob'. The third stage, after 'deployment of riot-control forces', was the use of water cannon, and the fourth stage, tear gas. (Several

E **BRAZILIAN CENTURION RIOT CONTROL VEHICLE**

The Centurion is one of the most powerful riot-control assets in the arsenal of the Batalhão de Polícia de Choque (Battalion of Special Forces, or BPChoque), a military police unit operating in Rio de Janeiro. The formation specializes in handling high-risk civil disturbances, and the Centurion provides the means to deliver riot units securely into dangerous locations. The 6x6 vehicle has interior seating for up to 14 personnel, plus the two crew in the heavily armoured front cab. Access to the rear cab is via single side doors or double rear doors. The body is armoured against small-arms threats, and a single water cannon over the cab can engage targets out beyond 30m. The vehicle features both front and rear dozer blades for obstacle clearance, and all windows have hinged wire-mesh protection. To aid with all-round surveillance, the vehicle has a roof-mounted viewing turret, plus a spotlight and surveillance camera.

Riot trucks are manufactured with varying degrees of sophistication. Here we see a fairly basic design in Harare, Zimbabwe in 2008, consisting of a commercial truck fitted with a large open-topped armoured body. The sides are angled to prevent people climbing on board and to provide some measure of mine-blast protection. (Press Association)

more steps follow, ending up with deploying all 'available unit fire power with the intent of producing extensive casualties'.)

Alongside the military RCVs used around the world, police water-cannon units were becoming the primary force option for many security forces. Such vehicles were deployed on an almost daily basis on the streets of Northern Ireland. As an operational example – and it is only one example amongst hundreds – on 5 August 1969 Belfast was blighted by another night of strife. Police were attacked with more than 30 petrol bombs and hundreds of missiles, thrown by some 1,000 residents who had poured out onto the streets. The rioters also erected roadblocks and obstacles to prevent the free movement of security forces. For a time it seemed as if the police and army were losing control, but eventually water cannon were deployed, along with an armoured truck designed to push aside the barriers. The jets from the water cannon broke up the crowds and managed to quench some of the street fires, while the armoured truck formed a protective shield behind which police could advance through the barricades.

Northern Ireland became a virtual laboratory for riot control until the 1990s. South Africa and many South American countries went through similar experiences. As time went on, however, many governments became increasingly

BELOW:
A militarized response. Mexican forces of the 12th Mechanized Regiment, deployed in US M20 Armoured Utility Cars, confront strikers in Oaxaca, Mexico, on 25 March 1952. (Press Association)

BELOW RIGHT: An Egyptian armoured personnel carrier in Cairo, 1986. Egypt has relied heavily on APCs for riot control. The vehicle here is a Spanish BMR-600, a 6x6 infantry fighting vehicle manufactured in the 1970s. It has a two-man crew plus space for 11 other occupants. (Press Association)

sensitive to the perception of how riots were handled, not just whether the riot control was effective. This emerging awareness also had an effect on how RCVs have been developed and deployed. In South Africa, for example, the Casspir was so ubiquitous in its township deployments by the apartheid regime that over time it became virtually synonymous with apartheid itself. (An article in the *LA Times* in 1989 referred to a car bumper sticker in South Africa that said 'Casspir – The unfriendly ghost'.) The Casspirs would be used to deploy police quickly and aggressively against rioters and their barricades (typically of burning tyres), the security troops inside either using the firing ports or roof hatches to deliver fire ranging from rubber bullets to live ammunition. As noted above, once the apartheid era ended, the new government steadily removed the old Casspirs from its police stocks.

Riot-control tactics even in developed states today can be fairly blunt, depending on the resources. Vehicles are typically used first to intimidate crowds by their presence (this frequently does not work), and then to disperse the crowds either by driving through them to split their concentration or by deploying water cannon and tear gas. They also attempt to make fast deployments of riot troops to apprehend key rioters. In return, the rioters respond with all manner of innovation: thick cables stretched across streets to snag personnel in hatches; burning pots of paint; beer barrels rolled under the chassis; wooden boards studded with nails to puncture tyres. Each innovation of the rioters feeds into the tactics of the RCV units, as does the spectrum of non-lethal weapon systems available. For example, since the 1980s, water cannon have been used to spray protesters with a semi-permanent coloured dye. The purpose of the dye is straightforward – what easier way to identify a rioter after the event than if they are highlighted with a deep shade of purple, green or blue? The delivery system for the dye is simple – the operator introduces the dye into the flow from the water cannon, and directs the coloured spray at the mass

The National Guard was frequently deployed in riot-control duties in the United States during the 1960s, often in the M113 APC, seen here on 27 July 1964 in Rochester, New York. (Press Association)

Bahrain, 2012. A water-cannon vehicle, probably of South Korean origin, is scorched by petrol bombs and daubed with graffiti. (Press Association)

of protestors. Note that the colour of the dye can have some important cultural implications. In India, for example, the police are advised against using purple dyes during the colourful festival of Holi, held in February or early March.

Dyes have been used extensively in riots over the last 30 years, in places such as Hungary, Indonesia and Israel. For example, on 23 October 2006, about a thousand protesters gathered in Budapest to make anti-government demonstrations on the 50th anniversary of the Hungarian uprising. The protest quickly turned ugly, as 150 police, supported by a helicopter and three water-cannon vehicles, moved in to confront the crowd, who in turn replied with bottles and rocks. Tear gas was fired, and as the violence intensified the police also shot rubber bullets, which inflicted some head injuries. Then three water-cannon vehicles, each with two cab-mounted nozzles, moved forward against the crowd in a unified front, spraying the protestors with a combination of blue and green dyed water. The riot was quashed within the day, and some of the now-colourful rioters were apprehended.

The dye system has proved effective, but is also predictably controversial. There have been reports of some dyes containing toxic, even carcinogenic properties, or at least causing skin irritations. Overall, it must be acknowledged that the employment of water cannon, while by no means rare, has become less common in the 2000s, particularly in Western Europe and the United States. (There are notable exceptions – according to a

CLASH IN SANTIAGO, 2012

In September 2012, in Santiago, Chile, a student demonstration in favour of education reform spiralled into a violent day of protest. As riot police moved in to clear the streets, the protestors responded with missiles of various power and type, and paint bombs were thrown at police vehicles. Here we see a Chilean police water cannon in operation against a group of protestors. The vehicle is the Rosenbauer RWD-6500, Rosenbauer being one of the world's leading manufacturers of firefighting and specialist emergency vehicles. The vehicle clearly shows the marks of the riot, but the jet spray has literally blasted a rioter off his feet. The vehicle has two water jets, staggered at opposite corners of the cabin to provide 360-degree vehicle protection, and the force of the stream can be varied by the operator.

Belfast, January 2013. Riot police forces gather to repel a hostile crowd. The water-cannon units are composite vehicles: coachworks by Somati (a Belgian company), the frame by Ginaf and the lorry parts from DAF. The protective systems came from companies in Holland and England. (Press Association)

Guardian report of April 2014, Belgian police deploy water-cannon vehicles roughly twice a week at football matches and demonstrations, although the water jet is turned on only about once a month.) Partly the reason is tactical. Water cannon can certainly subdue and break up a crowd, but as the range of the jet extends it may do little more than provide a soaking, which is not necessarily a potent dissuader for the rioters. At close ranges, however, the jets can easily slam a person into the ground if he or she receives the full force of the jet, even if the operator has the jet on its lowest pressure. A British government report in 2013 concluded that there was 'good evidence ... to indicate that serious injuries have been sustained by people subjected to the force of water cannon', these injuries including concussion, broken bones (from falls) and long-term balance problems resulting from the forced ingress of water into the ears. A German man,

A Mercedes-Benz NG 2628 Wasserwerfer 9000 water-cannon vehicle. Several second-hand versions of this particular vehicle have recently been purchased by the Metropolitan Police in the UK, in expectation of future disturbances in the British capital. (Sicherlich)

Dietrich Wagner, 69, was blinded in one eye when hit full in the face by a water jet in 2010.

There is also the issue of public image. In the United States in particular, the images of water cannon spraying down civil-rights protesters during the 1960s has left a stigma over the systems, and hence they are used infrequently. In the UK, the British police forces have conducted extensive enquiries into the applications of water cannon, with controversial conclusions. The debate was sparked by the Metropolitan Police in 2014 advocating that water cannon be purchased and ready in the British capital, in preparation for future civil disturbances. The Met's loss of control of the streets during riots in 2011 compelled them to look at greater force options, despite the fact that in the UK water cannon was authorized for use only in Northern Ireland. The intended purchase was the German Wasserwefer 9000, a 30-tonne vehicle with a 9,000-litre capacity water tank feeding two jet nozzles, powered by an FPN 15-2000-2 centrifugal fire pump.

Five of the six largest police forces in the UK rejected the need for the vehicles, both on tactical and financial grounds. Some senior officers from forces such as West Midlands, Merseyside and Greater Manchester expressed scepticism that water cannon actually help to control rioters, instead forcing them to disperse and then form up elsewhere. There was also the suggestion that such vehicles actually increase the severity of rioting, as their presence creates a heightened tension between rioters and police. Yet at the time of writing, the London Mayor, Boris Johnson, has accepted three of the vehicles into the ranks of the Metropolitan Police.

In the previous section, we also looked at some of the more modern weapon systems that are now coming into use with security forces. The ADS system, for example, was deployed to Afghanistan in 2010 with the US

An Israeli border police AIL Storm vehicle deploys a riot squad in Hebron, 2013. The Storm is a variant of the Wrangler Jeep, and the RCV version features polycarbonate shielding along the roof and windows, plus gun ports. (Press Association)

This striking image shows the conditions in which an RCV must operate. This Chilean vehicle is drenched in paint, and missiles litter the ground around it, although the bodywork looks relatively undamaged. (Davidlohr Bueso)

Army. For reasons unknown, however, the vehicle was not used and was quickly withdrawn from the theatre. Speculation abounds about the reason for this withdrawal. Some sources have suggested that the ADS beam is weakened in practical theatre environmental conditions, as it has to pass through dust and adverse weather. Others suggest that the world just simply is not ready to see US forces essentially microwaving large crowds of civilians. Whatever the truth, the theoretically persuasive nature of the system means that operational use is certainly possible in the near future, if only in non-US hands.

One new vehicular weapon system that has received a combat outing is Israel's 'The Scream' system. In September 2001 it was deployed against demonstrators near the West Bank village of Bil'in. Witnesses to the incident spoke of people clutching their ears and then dropping to the ground as their balance was affected. Its incorporation into the Israeli arsenal was part of a search for crowd-control measures at vulnerable border outposts. If it is as effective as initial reports seem to suggest, it could become a staple riot-control response in future decades.

G

WEST BANK, 2013

If a riot-control vehicle does not have strong defensive equipment, then it must rely more on its mobility to survive a civil disturbance. Here we see a police Sandcat vehicle making a hasty retreat along a street in the West Bank, under a shower of missiles from local youths. The vehicle has already fired gas grenades from its roof-mounted launcher, the gas lacing the street. The Sandcat (or Caracal) is made by the Plasan concern of Israel as a versatile multipurpose armoured vehicle for military and security use. It is a 4x4 vehicle with a crew of between four and eight personnel, depending on the configuration. The body is fully armoured and can be upgraded with a field package to enhance the protection. For policing civil disturbances, the Sandcat can be fitted with grenade launchers, bull bars and loud speakers. It can also be fitted with a fire-suppression system. Powered by a 6-litre V8 diesel, the Sandcat has excellent power and manoeuvrability, characteristics that have made it popular with its users.

CONCLUSION

As part of the research for this book, the author spoke with Len Mellett, Head of Innovation for the Paramount Group and the lead designer behind the company's Maverick vehicle. Len provided some invaluable insight into the failings of early generations of RCVs:

> Historically and traditionally what has happened is that police and anti-riot agencies, when they've had a requirement for vehicles, have tended to look at what is commercially available and then try to modify and increase the capability of a civilian vehicle. Typically this results in you having a product that is non-optimal. It is now totally overloaded, because it has been modified to do something it was never designed to do, so all your reliability goes down and your life-cycle costs go up. But usually to fix this problem very few people make the conscious decision to stop the game, define and start from first principles focused on what they actually require and invest the money up front, so at the end of the day life-cycle costs are down and they have a purpose-designed vehicle.
>
> Look at up-armoured Toyota Landcruisers, or up-armoured Land Rovers, the light delivery vehicles and light commercial trucks that have been beefed up with armour plate with changed paintwork and used as security vehicles... What you end up with is an overloaded vehicle with ballistic windows that is non-optimal. Then you also use drivers who are not trained in these vehicles, who abuse them, so you get low reliability.

The situation described by Len has been a classic failure of many RCVs throughout history. Only in relatively recent years have designers really thought seriously about the visual, political and operational integrity of RCVs. Producing a vehicle that satisfies all the requirements is far from easy, as Len continues:

> What you really have to do is to look at the vehicle systematically. If there is a disturbance, the first and most important thing is your information system. In other words: What has caused this? Who's behind this? How bad can this get? You ask these questions before you even go to the crowd... Then you want to design a vehicle that from a distance can change the behaviour and attitude of the crowd. It can't look too aggressive, but it must look mean enough to say 'don't try and tackle me or you're going to get hurt'. It's a fine line to get that design right. Then of course you have to say to yourself: 'How do we keep the crowd away?' Do you use tear gas, do you use rubber bullets, do you use water, do you use dye? And what information do you need after the encounter? So you've got to design a system that can hold 20,000-litres of water, stand there for two days, record everything and mark the people, but if you design a vehicle like that you end up with a huge vehicle that can't go anywhere. So there are some trade-offs with optimization.

What this passage acknowledges is that the true RCV is not a blunt instrument. Instead it is an advanced piece of technology designed to withstand and confront some of the most intense threat conditions to be found anywhere. To achieve the optimal RCV design is no mean feat, requiring a complex series of challenges that involve cultural and political

A Turkish water-cannon vehicle, manufactured by Katmerciler Arac Ustu Ekipman Sanayi & Ticaret AS (KATMR), here seen combatting demonstrations in Ankara in May 2014. It has a single top-mounted water jet, capable of firing pulses or solid jets. (Press Association)

considerations as well as mechanical ones. The best examples of RCVs certainly have the power to influence mass protests. The worst usually end up burning on the street.

FURTHER READING

Arden, Michael et al. (2008). *Metropolitan Police Images: Motor Vehicles*. Chichester: Phillimore & Co.

Foss, Christopher F. (1984). *Jane's Light Tanks and Armoured Cars*. London: Jane's Publishing.

Gates, Daryl with Diane K. Shah (1992). *Chief: My Life in the LAPD*. New York: Bantam Books.

McNab, Chris (2009). *Deadly Force: From the Wild West to the Streets of Today*. Oxford: Osprey Publishing.

McNab, Chris (2003). *Military Vehicles*. London: Amber Books.

Mechanics and Handicraft magazine (May 1938).

Ripley, Tim (1993). *Security Forces in Northern Ireland 1969–92*. Oxford: Osprey Publishing.

Shapiro, Larry (1999). *Special Police Vehicles*. Osceola, WI: MBI.

INDEX

References to images and plates are in **bold**.

Active Denial System (ADS) 11, 31–32, **33** (D, 32), 34, 43–44
Afghanistan 32, 43
air conditioning 19, 20
anti-riot systems 5
apartheid 22, 39
armoured cars 6, 14, 15, 21–22; Shorland 19–20, **21**
armoured personnel carriers (APCs) 10, 14, 21, 38; M113: 4, 35, 36, **39**; S55: 20; Saracen 16, 18, 19
armoured personnel vehicles (APVs): Shorts 20

Bahrain **4, 40**
barricades 4, 15, 18, 38, 39
bean-bag bullets 34
Beit Alpha Technologies (BAT) 23–24, 26
Belfast **20, 21**, 38, **42**
Belgium 42
Berlin 11
bodywork 5, 7, 9, **17** (A1, 16)
bombs 16
Brazil 14, **37** (E, 36)
British Army 18, 20, 21
bulkheads 16
bull bars 5, **17** (A1, 16), 18, 20

cabins 5, 22, 23
cameras 26, 34
chemical agents 10
Chile **5, 41** (F, 40) **44**
civil-rights protestors 13, 43
closed-circuit TV (CCTV) 26, 30
Cold War 11–14
comfort 26
Commer 8–9
computerized control systems 26, 27
Council for Scientific and Industrial Research (CSIR) 22
CR spray 10
crowd control 4, 5, 9, 39
CS gas 10, 16, **17** (A1, 16)

Daimler 15
Desert Wolf 34
Detroit 35, 36
drones 34
dye 24, 39–40

Eastern Europe 11
Egypt 6, 14, 38
Emergency Service Division (ESU) 8, 34
energy beams 11
engines 6, 9, 11, 12, 15, 16, 18, 19, 23
explosive ordnance disposal (EOD) 18, 30

fire **4, 5**
fire engines 12, 13, **14**
fire-extinguishing systems 16, 20, 21, 23, 30
floodlighting 26
foam 18, 24, 26

gangsters 6
Great Britain 8–9, 12, 14, 43; and Northern Ireland 15–16, 18–21

Hanover **36**
heating 20
High Mobility Multipurpose Wheeled Vehicle ('Humvee') 32, **33** (D, 32)

Hong Kong 8–9
Hungary 35, 40

improvised explosive devices (IEDs) 15, 18, 22, 30, 32
India 40
Indonesia 40
infantry fighting vehicles (IFVs) 4
injuries 42–43
internal security vehicle (ISV) 30
Iraq 32
Irish Civil War (1922–23) 6
Israel 23, 32, 34, 40, **43, 44, 45** (G, 44)

Jelcz 12
Johnson, Boris 43

ladders 8
laminated glass 22
Land Rover 19, 20, 21
landmines 22
long-range acoustic device (LRAD) 34
Los Angeles 35, 36
loudspeakers 11, 23, 34

Mayer 12, 22
Mechem Vehicles 22
Mellett, Len 46
Mercedes 11
Metropolitan Police 43
Mexico 38
microwave beams 5
military armoured vehicles 14–15
military forces 6, 10
missiles 8, 9, 14, 38
mobile adjustable ramp system (MARS) 30
Molotov cocktails 14

National Guard 4, **14**, 35, **39**
New Jersey 35
New York City Police Department (NYPD) 7, 8
Newark 35
non-lethal weaponry 9–11, 39
Northern Ireland 6, **13**, 15–16, 18–21, 22, 38
nuclear, biological and chemical (NBC) suites 14

obstacle removal 18, 20, 23, 26, 31
OMON security force 23

PA systems 20, 26
paintball guns 34
Palestine 6, 34
Paramount Group 46
pepper spray 24
Poland 12, 34
police vehicles 6–7
powerplants 22
Prohibition, the 6–7
psychological tools 11, 34
public image 22, 43

radios 6–7
rapid intervention water cannon (RIWC) 30–31
reconnaissance 15
riot-control agents (RCAs) 10
riot control vehicles (RCVs) 4–6, 7–8; Casspir 22–23, **25** (B2, 24) 39; Centurion **37** (E, 36); Czech OKV-P **17** (A2, 16); Hotspur 21; Humber Pig **17** (A1, 16), 18–19, **20**; Hydromil 12; INKAS **27**, 31; Land Rover

Tangi **13**, 21; Lavina (Avalanche) 23, **25** (B1, 24); Locomotors Talon 26; Nonqai 23; Paramount Group Maverick **12**, 26, 27, **28–29** (D, 28) 30–31, 46; Saladin 15–16; 'Scream, The' 34, 44; Simba 21; SK-2: 11–12; TAM 110: **35**; Wasserwefer 9000: **42**, 43; see also armoured cars; armoured personnel carriers
riot screens 18
riots 4, 5, 35–36, 39, 43
Rolls-Royce 6, 7, 15, 16
Royal Ulster Constabulary (RUC) 18, 19, 20, 21
rubber bullets 9, 10, 23, 40
Russia 23, **25** (B1, 24); see also Soviet Union

Santiago **41** (F, 40)
scout cars 14, 35
searchlights 8, 11
seating 8, 16, 22, 26
security forces 38–39
six-wheel drive 15, 16
skunk spray 34
'Socialist Water Jet' 11
sonic and ultrasound weapons (SUWs) 5, 11
South Africa 22–23, **25** (B2, 24), 27–28, 34, 38–39
Soviet Union 11–12, 14, 35
speed 6, 11, 15, 18, 20
student demonstrations **41** (F, 40)
surveillance systems 5, 11, 15, 26, 27
SWAT APC 30

tailboards 18
tanks 4, 14, 35, 36
tear gas 5, 14, 23, 24, 38, 39, 40
threat responses 7
'Thunder Blaster' 34
Tiananmen Square 14
Tunaya, Victorino L. 7
Turkey **9, 47**
turrets 7, 10, 11, 19
tyres 5, 11, 20, 26, 30

Ukraine 10
Ulster Defence Force (UDF) 19, 20
United States of America 13, 14, 43; and police vehicles 6–8; and riots 4, 35–36
US Army 13, **33** (D, 32), 36, 38, 43–44

Vehicle Protection Kit (VPK) 20–21
ventilation 20
vision slots 9, 16, 20, 22

water cannons 5, **9**, 10, 11–13, 18, 22, 23, 24, 26, 38, 39–40, 42–43; see also rapid intervention water cannon
Watts Riots (1965) 35, 36
WaveStun 32
weaponry: cannons 14, 15, 16; grenades 10, 26, 30; L5A1 guns 15; machine guns 6, **7**, 15, 16, 27, 30; pump-action shotguns 8; rocket-propelled grenades (RPGs) 18; smoke grenades 16, 20, 23; sub-machine guns 8
weight 18, 21
West Germany 12
wheelbases 5
windows 5, 9, 11, 20, 23, 26
windscreens 8, 20
World War I 6, **10**
World War II 6
Zimbabwe **38**